¿Qué hay debajo de la cama?

Mick Manning y Brita Granström

planetainfantil

¿Qué hay debajo de la cama?

Allí abajo hay tablones de
madera... y polvo.

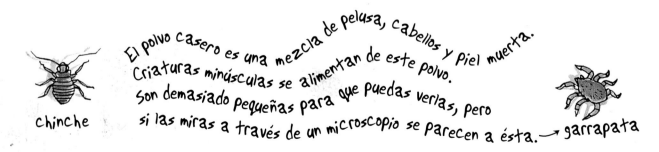

El polvo casero es una mezcla de pelusa, cabellos y piel muerta.
Criaturas minúsculas se alimentan de este polvo.
Son demasiado pequeñas para que puedas verlas, pero
si las miras a través de un microscopio se parecen a ésta. → garrapata

chinche

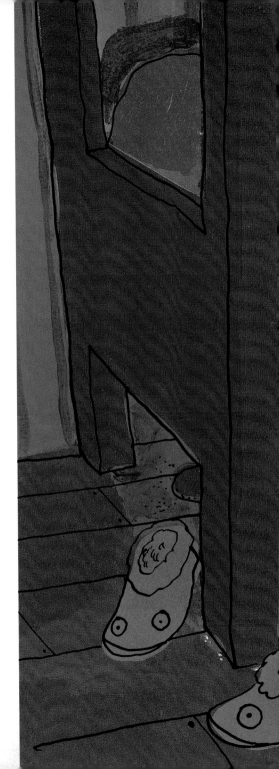

¿Qué hay debajo de la cama y de los tablones de madera?

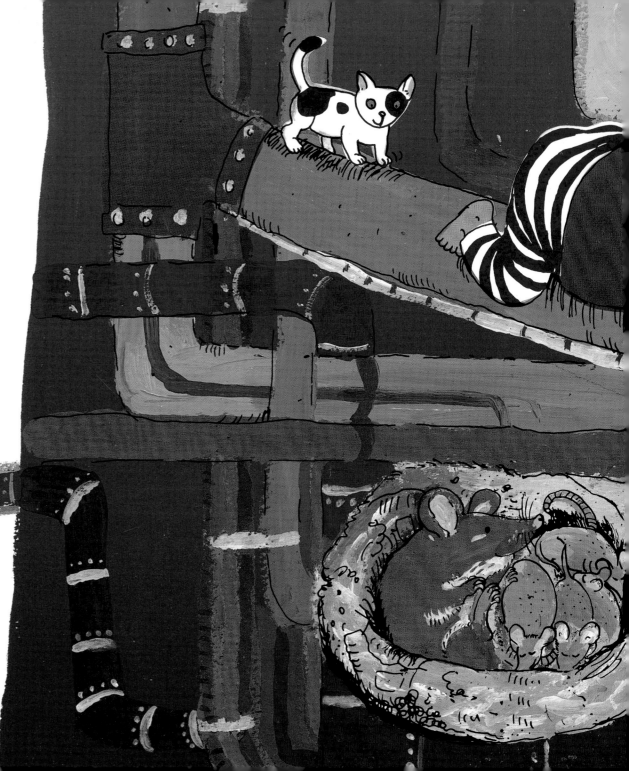

Hay cables y tubos debajo del piso y detrás de las paredes. Transportan la electricidad, el gas y el agua por toda la casa. Los tubos de desagüe sacan el desperdicio de los baños y de las cocinas.

Algunos tubos de agua han sido forrados para aislarlos...

El aislamiento mantiene caliente el agua dentro de los tubos.

Allí abajo hay cables y tubos, cables eléctricos y tubos de agua caliente en los que un ratón ha hecho su nido.

5

¿Qué hay debajo de la cama, de los tablones de madera, de los cables y tubos y del nido del ratón?

Un árbol tiene más o menos el mismo número de raíces bajo el suelo, como de ramas en la superficie.
Las raíces de las plantas crecen hacia dentro de la tierra para buscar su comida y el agua que necesitan.

6

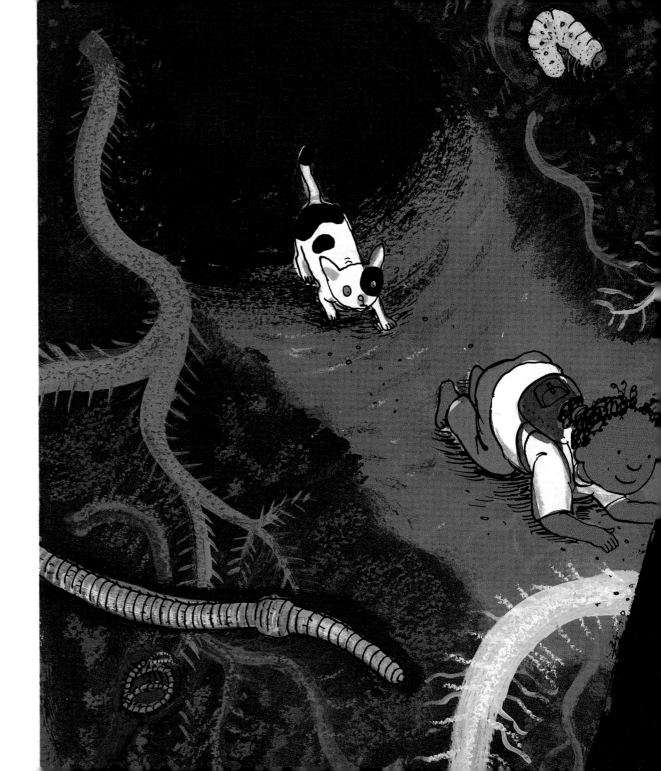

El suelo fértil está formado por partículas de roca mezcladas con aire, agua y hojas secas...

El suelo fértil es el hogar de muchas pequeñas criaturas.

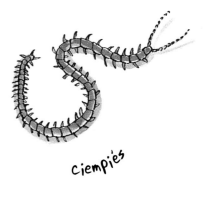

ciempiés

gusano de tierra

larva de escarabajo

Allí abajo hay suelo fértil y raíces de plantas, donde viven gusanos y animalitos minúsculos.

Qué hay debajo de la cama, de los tablones de madera, de los cables y tubos, del nido del ratón, del suelo fértil y las raíces?

Reina: pone todos los huevos.

Trabajadoras: son hembras que hacen todo el trabajo de la colonia; buscan la comida, cuidan los huevecillos y a los bebés.

Zángano: son machos que solo viven lo suficiente para ayudar a la reina a poner sus huevos

Las hormigas construyen sus casas debajo de la tierra, además de largos túneles con dormitorios, guarderías y basureros.

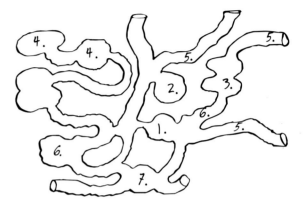

1. La reina con los huevecillos
2. La reina con las larvas
3. Crisálida
4. Las hormigas salen de los huevecillos
5. Las trabajadoras consiguen la comida
6. Las crisálidas y las larvas son trasladadas por las trabajadoras
7. Basurero

Allí abajo hay hormigas, una colonia de hormigas trabajadoras.

¿Qué hay debajo de la cama, de los tablones de madera, de los cables y tubos, del nido del ratón, del suelo fértil y las raíces y de la colonia de hormigas?

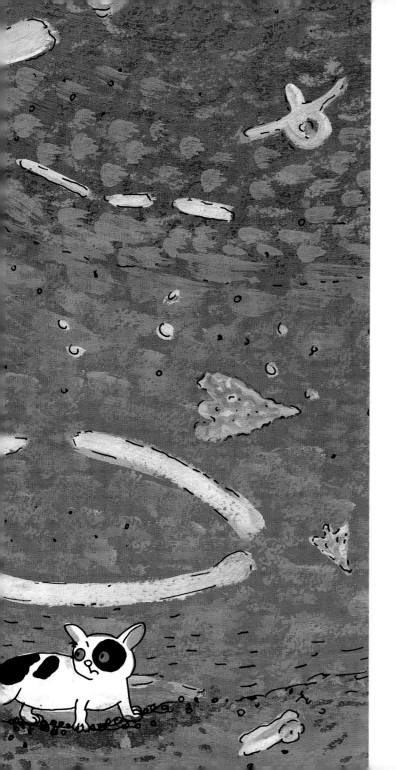

un horno antiguo

Barro: Es un tipo de roca suave, húmeda y pegajosa.

El barro se endurece cuando se calienta en un horno especial para fabricar alfarería.

De la tierra se extrae el barro para hacer platos, tazas, platones y muchas otras cosas.

un horno moderno

Allí abajo hay barro, huesos y puntas de flecha, que pertenecieron a personas que vivieron hace muchos, muchos años.

11

¿Qué hay debajo de la cama, de los tablones de madera, de los cables y tubos, del nido del ratón, del suelo fértil y las raíces, de la colonia de hormigas y del barro?

Muchas ciudades del mundo han ahorrado espacio al construir trenes subterráneos que trasladan a los pasajeros muy por debajo de la superficie.
Largas escaleras eléctricas van de la superficie a las plataformas.

Allí abajo hay un túnel, un túnel oscuro y ruidoso por el que circulan los trenes subterráneos.

13

¿Qué hay debajo de la cama, de los tablones de madera, de los cables y tubos, del nido del ratón, del suelo fértil y las raíces, de la colonia de hormigas, del barro y del ruidoso túnel?

un dinosaurio muere...

luego de millones de años se convierte en fósil.

Los fósiles son restos endurecidos de animales o plantas prehistóricos. Al comprimirse con la grava y con la arena, se convierten en piedra.

14

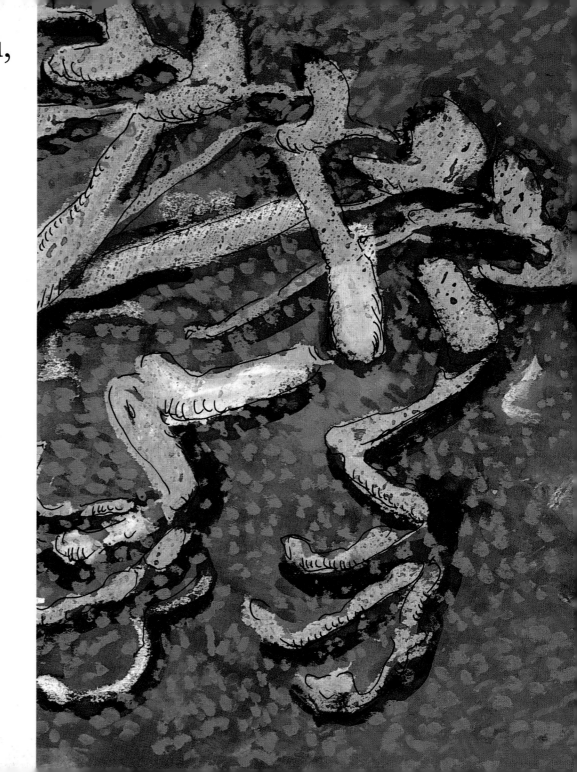

Podrías encontrar un fósil tú mismo observando piedras y guijarros.

Allí hay un dinosaurio, un fósil de dinosaurio enterrado entre varias capas de piedra.

15

¿Qué hay debajo de la cama, de los tablones de madera, de los cables y tubos, del nido del ratón, del suelo fértil y las raíces, de la colonia de hormigas, del barro, del ruidoso túnel y del fósil de dinosaurio?

Los pueblos prehistóricos que vivieron hace miles de años a menudo habitaban en cuevas. En las paredes dejaron pinturas de los animales que cazaban...

Con el agua, que escurre gota a gota acumulando minúsculas partículas de piedra, se forman piedras filosas en el techo y en el suelo de la cueva. Reciben el nombre de estalactitas y estalagmitas.

estalactita

estalagmita

Cuando el río se seca deja formada una cueva.

Poza: Lugar por donde escurría el antiguo río.

Boca de la cueva
Lugar por donde corría el antiguo río

Cuando el río se seca deja una cueva.

Allí abajo hay una cueva secreta, una cueva con pinturas prehistóricas en las paredes.

17

¿Qué hay debajo de la cama, de los tablones de madera, de los cables y tubos, del nido del ratón, del suelo fértil y las raíces, de la colonia de hormigas, del barro, del ruidoso túnel, del fósil de dinosaurio y de la cueva secreta?

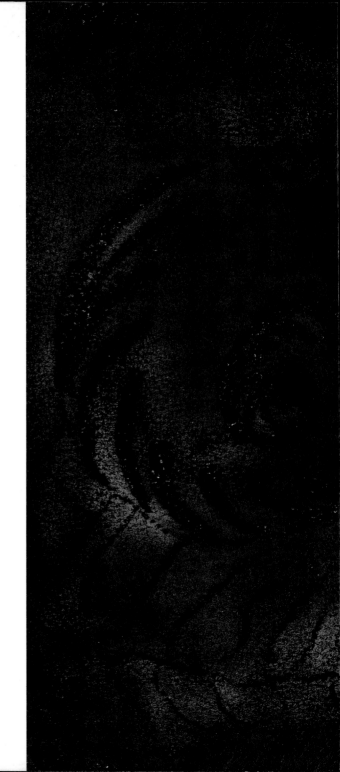

Bosques pantanosos quedaron enterrados por varias capas de lodo hace 300 millones de años y formaron los árboles fosilizados que se convirtieron en carbón.

El carbón se puede usar para hacer fogatas y producir electricidad.

Las minas de carbón son peligrosas. Deben cavarse profundos agujeros y túneles en la tierra.

Hace unos 100 años se usaban caballitos para que jalaran los carros de carbón. Incluso se enviaba a trabajar a las minas a niños pequeños.

Los mineros usan cascos para proteger su cabeza.

Allí abajo hay una mina de carbón, una vieja mina de carbón, en la que máquinas oxidadas reposan en la oscuridad y pueden encontrarse helechos fosilizados.

¿Qué hay debajo de la cama, de los tablones de madera, de los cables y tubos, del nido del ratón, del suelo fértil y las raíces, de la colonia de hormigas, del barro, del túnel ruidoso, del fósil de dinosaurio, de la cueva secreta y de la mina de carbón?

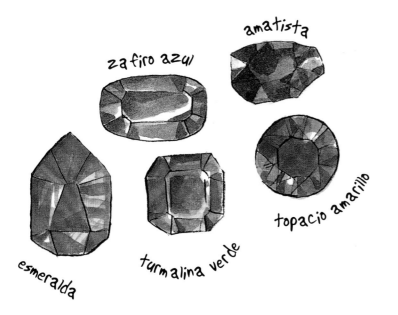

amatista

zafiro azul

topacio amarillo

esmeralda

turmalina verde

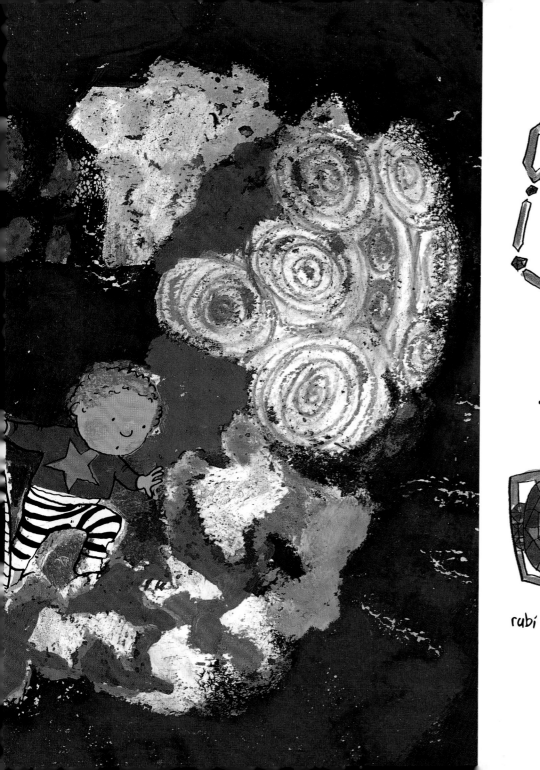

Muy profundo, por debajo de la roca dura, hace tanto calor que todo se funde. Cuando esto ocurre se forma oro, plata y piedras preciosas.

El oro y las piedras preciosas son extraídos de la tierra en las minas y son cortados en formas especiales para convertirlos en "joyas".

oro

plata

sircón verde

diamantes

rubí

Allí abajo hay piedras y metales preciosos. Los cuarzos y las esmeraldas brillan en medio de la plata y el oro.

21

¿Qué hay debajo de la cama, de los tablones de madera, de los cables y tubos, del nido del ratón, del suelo fértil y las raíces, de la colonia de hormigas, del barro, del túnel ruidoso, del fósil de dinosaurio, de la cueva secreta, de la mina de carbón, de los metales y piedras preciosos?

erupción

respiradero

respiradero lateral

magma corriendo

tierra rocosa

capa de otras erupciones

cámara del magma

El magma es roca fundida que se encuentra a 700 kilómetros de profundidad.
¡Nunca nadie ha hecho un agujero que llegue hasta allá!
Sin embargo, la conocemos porque en ocasiones hace caminos para salir a la superficie através de fracturas de la capa terrestre.
Es lo que llamamos un volcán.

Allí abajo hay magma, roca fundida más caliente que agua hirviendo. Imagina un calor tan tremendo que puede fundir la roca.

23

¿Qué hay debajo de la cama, de los tablones de madera, de los cables y tubos, del nido del ratón, del suelo fértil y las raíces, de la colonia de hormigas, del barro, del túnel ruidoso, del fósil de dinosaurio, de la cueva secreta, de la mina de carbón, de los metales y piedras preciosos y del magma?

¡Allí abajo está el centro de la Tierra! Metal líquido, más caliente de lo que puedes imaginar, recubre un núcleo duro de hierro y níquel parecido a una gigantesca bola de cañón.

La bola de hierro y níquel está en el centro de la Tierra, exactamente igual que el hueso enmedio del durazno.

Viaje al centro de la Tierra.

De modo que...
el centro de la Tierra, el magma,
los metales y piedras preciosos,
una mina de carbón, una cueva
secreta, un fósil de dinosaurio, un
túnel ruidoso, barro, una colonia
de hormigas, raíces, suelo fértil,
un nido de ratón, tubos, cables y
tablones de madera
... ¡es lo que hay debajo de la cama!

raíces

hormigas

tablones de madera

cama

cables y tubos

suelo fértil

barro

túnel

fósil de dinosaurio

una cueva secreta

¿Qué hay debajo de la cama?

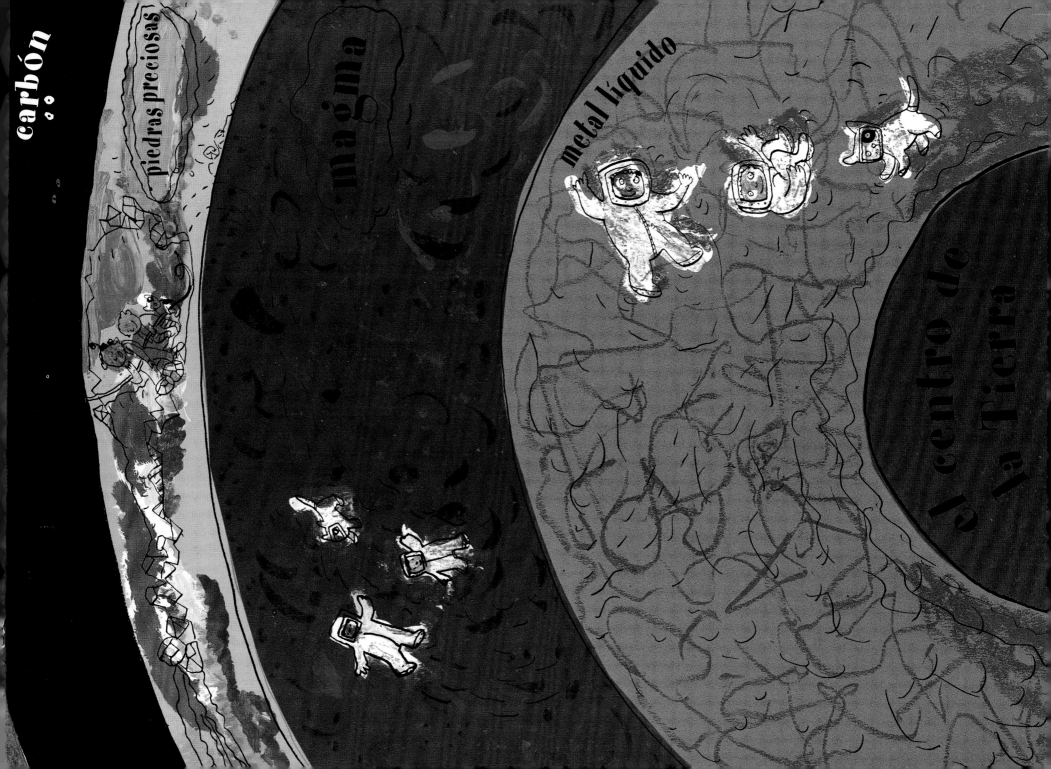

Palabras útiles

Animalitos minúsculos: Pequeñas criaturas, como insectos, gusanos y arañas (página 7).

Colonia: Un grupo de animales que viven y trabajan juntos (página 9).

Crisálida: Una etapa en la vida de los insectos, cuando comienzan a pasar de larvas a adultos (página 9).

Dinosaurios: Reptiles prehistóricos que vivieron en la Tierra hasta hace unos 65 millones de años (página 15).

Fósiles: Restos de plantas y animales prehistóricos que se han convertido en piedra (páginas 14-15).

Hierro y níquel: Los dos principales metales que forman el núcleo de la Tierra (página 25).

Larva: Una etapa en la vida de los insectos recién nacidos que han salido de su huevecillo (páginas 8-9).

Magma: Roca líquida a 700 kilómetros de profundidad (página 23).

Microscopio: Lentes de aumento especiales que pueden ayudarnos a ver cosas minúsculas al aumentar su tamaño (página 2).

Prehistórico: Nombre que damos a lo que ocurrió hace mucho tiempo, antes de que las personas comenzaran a escribir la historia (páginas 14, 16, 17).

Volcán: Lugar en la superficie de la Tierra donde la roca fundida, llamada magma, logra salir a la superficie. Los volcanes pueden estar sobre la tierra o bajo el mar y pueden desarrollarse como montañas o incluso como islas (página 23).

A Paula

Primera publicación por:
Franklin Watts
Copyright textos e ilustraciones (c)2002, Mick Manning y Brita Granström
Editor de la serie: Paula Borton

Primera edición en español por:
(c)2002, Distribuidora Planeta Mexicana, S. A. de C. V.
Av. Insurgentes Sur 1898, piso 11, Col. Florida
México D. F. 01030
Traducción al español: Eunice Cortés
ISBN: 970-690-588-X
Impreso en Singapur

DATE DUE

4/15/10	
2/24/11	
4/14/11	

This Place I Know

POEMS OF COMFORT

This Place I Know

POEMS OF COMFORT

Poems Selected by Georgia Heard

illustrations by
Eighteen Renowned Picture Book Artists

CANDLEWICK PRESS
CAMBRIDGE, MASSACHUSETTS

CONTENTS

A Note from the Author

During any difficult time, we all need a place where, as Faiz Ahmed Faiz writes in his poem "Song," "the heart [can] rest." Poetry has always offered comfort and consolation during sorrowful times, and reminded us of the places in our lives, inside and out, that can help us heal.

Several months ago, I was asked by my friend and colleague, who is superintendent of District 2 in Manhattan, to gather poems of comfort to read to the New York City children who witnessed the World Trade Center tragedy. What they saw from their classroom windows on the morning of September 11 changed their lives forever—as it changed all our lives as well.

As I read through poems for inclusion in this anthology, I kept asking myself one question: What words can comfort? I tried to choose poems that touch upon our feelings of fear and loss, remind us that we are not alone in despair, and assure us that dreams can be born even from tragedy.

My hope is that these beautiful and powerful poems and images will help children in New York City and all over the world—as Gwendolyn Brooks proclaims in "A Little Girl's Poem"—"to live," "to laugh," and "to sing" again.

Georgia Heard

THIS PLACE

There is this place I know
where children go to find
their deepest feelings
they look behind the trees
for hiding wants and angers
bashful joys
this place is quiet
no shouts may enter
no rolling laughter
but only silent tears
to carry the feelings
forward in waves
that wash the children
whole

Eloise Greenfield

Holly Meade

STARS

I like the way they looked down from the sky
And didn't seem to mind the way I cried.

And didn't say, "Now wipe away those tears,"
Or, "Tell us, tell us what's the matter here!"

But shining through the dark they calmly stayed,
And gently held me in their quiet way.

I felt them watching over me, each one—
And let me cry and cry till I was done.

Deborah Chandra

Yumi Heo

11

HOLD FAST YOUR DREAMS

Within your heart

Keep one still, secret spot

Where dreams may go,

And sheltered so,

May thrive and grow—

Where doubt and fear are not.

Oh, keep a place apart

Within your heart,

For little dreams to go.

Louise Driscoll

Hiroe Nakata

LULLABY

Will you hold me in your lap?

Will you cuddle me so tight?

Will you kiss my fearful brow,

And not turn off the light?

Will you soothe away my worry?

Will you sing the sweetest song?

Will you chase my fears away,

And rock me all night long?

Georgia Heard

Vivienne Flesher

A LITTLE GIRL'S POEM

Life is for me and is shining!
Inside me I
Feel stars and sun and bells singing.

There are children in the world
all around me and beyond me —
here, and beyond the big waters;
here, and in countries peculiar to me
but not peculiar to themselves.

I want the children to live and to laugh.
I want them to sit with their mothers
     and fathers
and have happy cocoa together.

I do not want
fire screaming up to the sky.
I do not want
families killed in their doorways.

Life is for us, for the children.
Life is for mothers and fathers,
life is for the tall girls and boys
in the high school on Henderson Street,
is for the people in Afrikan tents,

the people in English cathedrals,
the people in Indian courtyards;
the people in cottages all over the world.

Life is for us, and is shining.
We have a right to sing.

——————— Gwendolyn Brooks ———————

16

Giselle Potter

TROUBLE, FLY

Trouble, fly
out of our house.
We left the window
open for you.

Fly like smoke from a chimney.
Fly like the whistle from a train.
Fly far, far
away from my family,
mumbling in their sleep.

Trouble, fly.
Let our night
be a night of peace.

Susan Marie Swanson

Elisa Kleven

19

TO YOU

I think I could walk
through the simmering sand
if I held your hand.
I think I could swim
the skin shivering sea
if you would accompany me.
And run on ragged, windy heights,
climb rugged rocks
and walk on air:

I think I could do anything at all,
if you were there.

Karla Kuskin

William Steig

COMMITMENT IN A CITY

On the street we two pass.

I do not know you.

I did not see

if you are —

fat/thin,

dark/fair,

young/old.

If we should pass again

within the hour,

I would not know it.

Yet —

I am committed to

love you.

You are part of my city,

my universe, my being.

If you were not here

to pass me by,

a piece would be missing

from my jigsaw-puzzle day.

— Margaret Tsuda —

Jill McElmurry

23

HOLES

Strangest of gaps
their goneness—
mother, father, loved friends

the black holes
of the astronomer
are not more mysterious

this kind of hole
will not be filled
with candle flames
or even a thousand thoughts

the hole is inside us
it brims over
is empty and full at once.

—— Lillian Morrison ——

Shane W. Evans

STRENGTHEN THE THINGS THAT REMAIN

Rainbows still live in the sky and green grass
is growing everywhere. Clouds have familiar shapes
and sunsets have not changed color in a long time. Thunder
still follows lightning and spring comes after winter's
    misery.

A tree is still a tree and a rock is still a rock. A warbler
sings its familiar song and coyotes howl
in disconcerting harmony. Grasshoppers still hop

to their own music,
bees still buzz with excitement, and squirrels
still jump like acrobats. Mountains still contain mystery
and oceans surge with eternity. Bears still sleep in winter

and eagles fly higher than other birds. Snakes have an affinity
for the ground, while fish
are content in water. Patterns persist,
life goes on, whatever rises will converge.

Do what you will, but strengthen the things that remain.

Nancy Wood

Petra Mathers

Life is mostly froth and bubble,

Two things stand like stone;

Kindness in another's trouble,

Courage in your own.

A. L. Gordon

Laura McGee Kvasnosky

SONG

Pain will cease, do not grieve, do not grieve —

Friends will return, the heart will rest, do not grieve, do not
     grieve —

The wound will be made whole, do not grieve, do not grieve —

Day will come forth, do not grieve, do not grieve —

The cloud will open, night will decline, do not grieve, do not
     grieve —

The seasons will change, do not grieve, do not grieve.

— Faiz Ahmed Faiz —

Vladimir Radunsky

DREAMS

Hold fast to dreams
For if dreams die
Life is a broken-winged bird
That cannot fly.

Hold fast to dreams
For when dreams go
Life is a barren field
Frozen with snow.

Langston Hughes

Matt Tavares

FROM SONG OF THE BROAD-AXE

What do you think endures?

Do you think a great city endures?

Or a teeming manufacturing state? or a prepared constitution? or
     the best built steamships?

Or hotels of granite and iron? or any chef-d'oeuvres of engineering,
     forts, armaments?

Away! these are not to be cherish'd for themselves,

They fill their hour, the dancers dance, the musicians play for
     them,

The show passes, all does well enough of course,

All does very well till one flash of defiance.

A great city is that which has the greatest men and women,

If it be a few ragged huts it is still the greatest city in the whole
     world.

Walt Whitman

Peter Sís

RING AROUND THE WORLD

Ring around the world
Taking hands together
All across the temperate
And the torrid weather.
Past the royal palm-trees
By the ocean sand
Make a ring around the world
Taking each other's hand;
In the valleys, on the hill,
Over the prairie spaces,
There's a ring around the world
Made of children's friendly faces.

Annette Wynne

Melissa Sweet

"Hope" is the thing with feathers—

That perches in the soul—

And sings the tune without the words—

And never stops—at all—

And sweetest—in the Gale—is heard—

And sore must be the storm—

That could abash the little Bird

That kept so many warm—

I've heard it in the chillest land—

And on the strangest Sea—

Yet, never, in Extremity,

It asked a crumb—of Me.

———— Emily Dickinson ————

G. Brian Karas

THE PEACE OF WILD THINGS

When despair for the world grows in me

and I wake in the night at the least sound

in fear of what my life and children's lives may be,

I go and lie down where the wood drake

rests in his beauty on the water, and the great heron feeds.

I come into the peace of wild things

who do not tax their lives with forethought

of grief. I come into the presence of still water.

And I feel above me the day-blind stars

waiting with their light. For a time

I rest in the grace of the world, and am free.

— Wendell Berry

Kevin Hawkes

THE BEGINNING

This is where it begins
like God really lives in New York
and he opens his hands, PRESTO!
there are subway trains
   churning through the dark,
and Brooklyn Bridge swaying
   all its lights like ribbons,
and buildings climbing the sky
   the clouds just near,
and sea lapping the docks
   where men bellow and yell.
And there are children in parks
   always on swings,
and dogs running underfoot
   like bits of escaped rug,
and museums full of bones, birds,
   paintings and teeth —
long ago and here and always
   He said,
"Here's New York!"

Ann Turner

Chris Raschka

About the Illustrators

Shane W. Evans

"My inspiration for creating this artwork came to me in thinking about the events of September 11 and the poem 'Holes' by Lillian Morrison. Like the person in my illustration, I often find myself using my hands to frame little sections of the world, creating an instant composition, a 'portable window' to look through. 'Holes' inspired in me the representation of something no longer there. I was in New York City during and after the tragedy and remember looking into the sky; the composition had changed completely and dramatically. It was daunting to put up my 'portable window' and not see something otherwise so familiar."

Vivienne Flesher

"As I was working on my piece for this book, I couldn't feel anything. I think I was numb from it all. But after I was done, I felt grateful to be able to join with these other fine artists in an attempt to help all those affected by the terrible events of September 11."

Kevin Hawkes

"Wendell Berry's poem 'The Peace of Wild Things' spoke very strongly to me. As a young man, whenever I felt sad or lonely, I went hiking in the woods or mountains. There is something very comforting, even magical, about walking slowly out of doors, trying to spot wildlife, or sitting quietly in tall grass, looking at the insects. Smelling the earth and hearing the sounds of nature are powerful reminders that life is good."

Yumi Heo

"Often, after September 11, I've found myself looking up at the night sky. The stars twinkle as usual, as they did a million years ago, as they did on September 11, and as they will tomorrow. Though something tremendous and sad has changed us all, I am comforted by the beauty of the night sky."

G. Brian Karas

G. Brian Karas has taken on many subjects in the books he has written and illustrated for children. This wide range represents his interest in portraying the humorous, frightened, adventurous, painful, brave, and tender moments that are childhood. Perhaps the most difficult for the artist was his contribution to this anthology. He says, "I wondered how an artist could provide comfort for the world's universal grieving for the tragic events of September 11, or any tragic event for that matter, with words or pictures. But I found that it was words and pictures that most comforted me during difficult times and maybe I could possibly help with my art. My hope is that it *will* — somewhere, to someone."

Elisa Kleven

"'Trouble, Fly,' by Susan Marie Swanson, resonates with me, as the narrator puts into words what I feel each night when I put my children to bed — my hope that 'this night,' and all future nights, will be peaceful for them and for all the innocent life that inhabits our gorgeous, one and only world." Elisa Kleven is the illustrator of many picture books, among them, *Abuela* by Arthur Dorros, *Our Big Home* by Linda Glaser, and her own *The Paper Princess, Sun Bread,* and *The Dancing Deer and the Foolish Hunter.* She lives in Albany, California, with her husband, daughter, son, and various pets.

Laura McGee Kvasnosky

"'Life is mostly froth and bubble,' by A. L. Gordon, is a simple poem that aligns kindness and courage. Reading it, I remembered a dream my sister and I shared when we were six and eight. We dreamed we were awakened by a gossamer lady and a huge lion sitting on our cedar chest. Although this was frightening, we both knew the lady was kind. To create the image for this poem, I folded the folktale of Androcles and the Lion into the dream."

Petra Mathers

"When I first read 'my' poem, 'Strengthen the Things That Remain' by Nancy Wood, I panicked. So much nature, all this harmony. Where was the peril? Where were the buildings? Then, one day, I noticed the shell that sits on my windowsill. It looked like the poem, like a monument to the things that remain."

Jill McElmurry

"As I read the poem 'Commitment in a City,' I thought of what I love best about city life: watching everyone, so different yet so close together, sharing an avenue, a sidewalk, or a patch of grass, doing the dances that city people do with or around each other as if they were choreographed. I've lived in coastal towns and mountain towns, in wide-open desert places and narrow, jungly canyons, but living in cities has taught me what it means to be human."

Holly Meade

"Finding a place to weep and wash your troubles away — what lovely images Eloise Greenfield's words bring to mind in 'This Place.' Perhaps some comfort can be found here, in the place where images and words come together."

Hiroe Nakata

"I was born in Japan and grew up there. Now I live in New York. On a quiet night, the moon makes me feel at home, no matter where I am. When I was little, the moonlight that came through my bedroom window brought many dreams to my sleepy head."

Giselle Potter

"I drew a lot as a child because that is what everyone around me did. Both my grandparents were painters and my grandfather always invited other people to add to his paintings." Giselle Potter's first illustration job was a drawing for the *New Yorker*. Her first children's book was *Mr. Semolina-Semolinus: A Greek Folktale;* she has illustrated eleven other children's books since then. Giselle Potter lives in New York's Hudson Valley.

Vladimir Radunsky

Vladimir Radunsky was born in Russia and has lived in New York City since 1982. He has illustrated many books for children, among them *The Maestro Plays* by Bill Martin Jr; *Yucka Drucka Droni* by Eugenia Radunsky; *An Edward Lear Alphabet,* in collaboration with Bagram Ibatoulline; *Discovery* by Joseph Brodsky; *Square Triangle Round Skinny; Table Manners,* which he co-wrote and co-illustrated with Chris Raschka; and *Howdi Do, Bling Blang,* and *My Dolly,* all written by Woody Guthrie.

Chris Raschka

"This beautiful poem, 'The Beginning' by Ann Turner, sent me to a beautiful spot I know, the middle of the Manhattan Bridge. There, with the trains to and from Brooklyn running by, I painted this picture of the southern tip of Manhattan, with the Brooklyn Bridge and the towers of Wall Street and even a glimpse of the Statue of Liberty — all bits of this place I know and love."

Peter Sís

Peter Sís is the author and illustrator of numerous award-winning books for children. He has lived in downtown Manhattan for almost twenty years with his wife and two children, though he says, "I continue to be amazed by the city of New York — every day I wake up to a new dream of a new world."

William Steig

William Steig is a renowned *New Yorker* artist and the creator of numerous picture books and novels, including *Sylvester and the Magic Pebble, The Amazing Bone, Dominic, Abel's Island, Doctor DeSoto,* and *Shrek!* Of his inspiration for his illustration in *This Place I Know,* William Steig says, "I remembered Kasha and Pearl, two good old canine friends."

Melissa Sweet

Melissa Sweet has illustrated many books for children, including the Pinky and Rex series by James Howe, *On Christmas Day in the Morning: A Traditional Carol* by John Langstaff, and *Girls Think of Everything: Stories of Ingenious Inventions by Women* by Catherine Thimmesh. An amateur astronomer, she finds a lot of comfort in the night sky and is currently building a Newtonian telescope. She lives with her family in Rockport, Maine.

Matt Tavares

"When I first read 'Dreams' by Langston Hughes, I thought of how the events of September 11, 2001, left many people feeling like the broken-winged bird mentioned in the poem. In my illustration, I wanted to show the joy that can come from holding fast to our dreams, and not allowing ourselves to be paralyzed by fear and negativity."

ACKNOWLEDGMENTS

"This Place" from *Under the Sunday Tree* by Eloise Greenfield. Text copyright © 1988 by Eloise Greenfield. Used by permission of HarperCollins Publishers.

"Stars" from *Balloons and Other Poems* by Deborah Chandra. Copyright © 1990 by Deborah Chandra. Reprinted by permission of Farrar, Straus and Giroux, LLC.

"Lullaby" by Georgia Heard. Copyright © 2001 by Georgia Heard. Reprinted by permission of the author.

"A Little Girl's Poem" from *Very Young Poets* by Gwendolyn Brooks. Copyright © 1983 by the David Company, Chicago.

"Trouble, Fly" from *Getting Used to the Dark* by Susan Marie Swanson. Text copyright © 1997 by Susan Marie Swanson. Reprinted by permission of DK Publishing Inc.

"To You" by Karla Kuskin. Copyright © 1987 by Karla Kuskin. Reprinted by permission of S©ott Treimel NY.

"Commitment in a City" from *Cry Love Aloud* by Margaret Tsuda. Copyright © 1972 by Margaret Tsuda. Reprinted by permission of the author. First published in *The Christian Science Monitor*.

"Holes" from *Overheard in a Bubble Chamber and Other Science Poems* by Lillian Morrison. Copyright © 1981 by Lillian Morrison. Used by permission of Marian Reiner for the author.

"Strengthen the Things That Remain" from *Sacred Fire* by Nancy Wood, illustrated by Frank Howell. Copyright © 1998 by Nancy Wood. Used by permission of Random House Children's Books, a division of Random House, Inc.

"Life is mostly froth and bubble" by A. L. Gordon from *Poems for Life*. Published by Arcade Publishing.

"Song" by Faiz Ahmed Faiz from *Poems for Life*. Published by Arcade Publishing.

"Dreams" from *The Collected Poems of Langston Hughes* by Langston Hughes. Copyright © 1994 by The Estate of Langston Hughes. Used by permission of Alfred A. Knopf, a division of Random House, Inc.

"What do you think endures?" from "Song of the Broad-Axe" in *Leaves of Grass* by Walt Whitman.

"Ring Around the World" from *All Through the Year* by Annette Wynne. Copyright 1932 by Annette Wynne. Used by permission of HarperCollins Publishers.

"'Hope' is the Thing with Feathers" from *The Poems of Emily Dickinson*, Thomas H. Johnson, ed., Cambridge, MA: The Belknap Press of Harvard University Press. Copyright © 1951, 1955, 1979 by the President and Fellows of Harvard College. Reprinted by permission of the publishers and the Trustees of Amherst College.

"The Peace of Wild Things" from *The Selected Poems of Wendell Berry* by Wendell Berry. Copyright © 1998 by Wendell Berry. Reprinted by permission of Counterpoint, a member of the Perseus Books Group.

"The Beginning" from *Street Talk* by Ann Turner. Text copyright © 1986 by Ann Turner. Reprinted by permission of Houghton Mifflin Company and Curtis Brown Ltd. All rights reserved.

For my mother and father,
with love
G. H.

Special thanks to Shelley Harwayne, Superintendent of District 2 in Manhattan,
who gave me the chance to be of service after September 11 by asking me to find poems of comfort
for the New York City schoolchildren; Kara LaReau, my editor at Candlewick Press,
who helped create a wider vision for this important project; and Dermot and Leo,
who give me comfort every day.

This collection copyright © 2002 by Georgia Heard
Poems copyright © year of publication by individual authors as noted in Acknowledgments
Illustration for "Holes" copyright © 2002 by Shane W. Evans. Illustration for "Lullaby" copyright © 2002 by Vivienne Flesher.
Illustration for "The Peace of Wild Things" copyright © 2002 by Kevin Hawkes. Illustration for "Stars" copyright © 2002 by Yumi Heo.
Illustration for "'Hope' is the thing with feathers" copyright © 2002 by G. Brian Karas. Illustration for "Trouble, Fly" copyright © 2002 by Elisa Kleven.
Illustration for "Life is mostly froth and bubble" copyright © 2002 by Laura McGee Kvasnosky.
Illustration for "Strengthen the Things That Remain" copyright © 2002 by Petra Mathers.
Illustration for "Commitment in a City" copyright © 2002 by Jill McElmurry. Illustration for "This Place" copyright © 2002 by Holly Meade.
Illustration for "Hold Fast Your Dreams" copyright © 2002 by Hiroe Nakata. Illustration for "A Little Girl's Poem" copyright © 2002 by Giselle Potter.
Illustration for "Song" copyright © 2002 by Vladimir Radunsky. Illustration for "The Beginning" copyright © 2002 by Chris Raschka.
Illustration for "From 'Song of the Broad-Axe'" copyright © 2002 by Peter Sís. Illustration for "To You" copyright © 2002 by William Steig.
Illustration for "Ring Around the World" copyright © 2002 by Melissa Sweet. Illustration for "Dreams" copyright © 2002 by Matt Tavares.

First edition 2002

Library of Congress Cataloging-in-Publication Data

This place I know : poems of comfort / selected by Georgia Heard ;
illustrations contributed by eighteen renowned children's book artists. —1st ed.
p.   cm.
ISBN 0-7636-1924-8
1. Children's poetry, American. I. Heard, Georgia.
PS586.3 .G74 2002
811.008'09282—dc21   2002017503

2 4 6 8 10 9 7 5 3

Printed in the United States of America

This book was typeset in Stempel Schneidler. The illustrations were done in various media.

Candlewick Press
2067 Massachusetts Avenue
Cambridge, Massachusetts 02140

visit us at www.candlewick.com